DATE DUE

APR 0 5 1990		
OCT 2 8 1990		
NOV 1 4 1990		
JAN 2 2 1991		
MAR 1 2 1992	OCT ~ 9 1992	
NOV 1 9 1992		
MAR 2 2 1993		
NOV 1 6 1993		
MAY 11 '95		
NOV 4 '98		
JUN 0 1 2004		

P9-CET-054

A New True Book

STORMS

By Ray Broekel

This "true book" was prepared
under the direction of
Illa Podendorf,
formerly with the Laboratory School,
University of Chicago

CHILDRENS PRESS, CHICAGO

The author has had firsthand experience in all the kinds of storms presented in this book.
He prefers the kinds having rainbows.

PHOTO CREDITS

Joseph A. DiChello, Jr — 2, 6,(middle), 8 (top), 14, 16, 22 (2 photos)

Julie O'Neil — 4

National Oceanic & Atmospheric Administration (NOAA) — 6 (top), 31, 32, 36, 39

Candee & Associates — 6 (bottom), 8 (bottom), 19, 33, 41

Reinhard Brucker — Cover, 10 (top), 13, 42

Lynn M. Stone — 10 (bottom)

M. Cole — 40

Marty Hanson — 20 (top)

Tom Winter — 20 (bottom)

Allan Roberts — 24, 28 (2 photos), 35 (2 photos)

James M. Mejuto — 27, 44   COVER — Rainbow after a storm

Library of Congress Cataloging in Publication Data

Broekel, Ray.
  Storms.

  (A New true book)
  Summary: Describes the weather conditions
that produce storms and the damage that can
be done by rain, snow, wind, dust, ice, thunder,
lightning, and hail.
  1. Storms — Juvenile literature. [1. Storms]
I. Title. II. Series.
QC941.3.B76   551.5'5   81-15455
ISBN 0-516-01654-7   AACR2

TABLE OF CONTENTS

Storm in Hawaii

4

STORMS

There are many kinds of storms. But each kind is different.

Have you ever been in a rainstorm?

Or in a snowstorm?

Or in a bad windstorm?

Sailboats need the wind.

Clothes can dry in the wind.

The wind can carry balloons high into the sky.

WIND

What is wind?

Wind is moving air.

You cannot see it. But you can see how it moves things.

You can feel it blowing against you.

Fair weather clouds

CLOUDS

What are clouds?

They are made up of tiny drops of water. Or tiny bits of ice. The bits are called ice crystals.

Some clouds look like puffs of cotton. You see them on nice days.

These clouds are called fair weather clouds.

Storm
clouds

10

Some clouds look dark.
One such kind looks big
and mean in the sky. It is
the thundercloud.

WARM AND COLD AIR

Suppose the air is warm. Then a storm may carry rain.

But suppose the air is cold. Then the storm may carry snow.

Storm clouds over Bryce Canyon National Park

Rainstorm in New York City

RAINSTORMS

Lots of rain may fall during a rainstorm.

A light rain is called a shower.

"April showers bring May flowers."

Winter in Vermont

16

SNOWSTORMS

Lots of snow may fall
during a snowstorm.
Roads are covered.

Sidewalks are covered.
Snowplows go to work.
Sometimes schools are closed because of a snowstorm.

Sometimes a light snow falls. Would you call this a snow shower?

Snowplow at work

Trees in a
wind storm

Dust devil, a small dust storm

WINDSTORMS

Sometimes a storm is just wind.

The wind may blow hard.

Some windstorms blow lots of dust about. Sometimes windstorms are called dust storms.

Ice storms cover everything with a thin sheet of ice.

SLEET

What is sleet?

Sleet is a mix of snow and rain.

Sleet forms a coat of ice on trees and streets. Everything is slippery.

Sleet storms may be called ice storms, too.

Thunderstorm

24

THUNDERSTORMS

There is a lot of rain
in thunderstorms.
Lightning can flash
across the sky.
Then you hear thunder.

LIGHTNING AND THUNDER

You can see lightning.
It makes a noise. The
noise is called thunder.
You see the lightning
first. Then you hear the
thunder.

Electrical thunderstorm over Tucson, Arizona

Most hail is small. But some hail may be as big
as an egg, as seen in the picture below.

HAILSTORMS

Sometimes hail falls in thunderstorms.

Raindrops fall through cold air. They turn into ice. They are now called hail.

The wind may toss the hail up and down in the cold air. The hail may get bigger.

HURRICANES

Hurricanes are big storms. They form over ocean water.

The winds are strong. The rains are heavy. Ocean waves are high.

These big storms wear out as they move over land.

Hurricane winds may
blow over trees.

Ocean waves are high in
hurricanes. The waves may
break up houses near the
coast.

Tornado near Enid, Oklahoma

Sky before a tornado

TORNADOES

A tornado is shaped like a funnel.

The winds in a tornado are very strong. They can suck things up from the ground.

Tornadoes are very
strong storms. But they do
not last long.

Their winds can rip up
houses and stores.

Tornado damage in Xenia, Ohio

Waterspouts near the Grand Bahama Islands

WATERSPOUTS

Tornadoes may form over water. Then the storms have a different name. They are called waterspouts.

BLIZZARDS

Blizzards are big snowstorms. The winds are strong. There is a lot of snow. The strong winds blow the snow about.

Eighteen-foot snowdrifts in Hamburg, New York

Sometimes the wind blows the snow into huge piles. These are called drifts.

Cars and trucks get
stuck.
People stay inside during
a blizzard.

Rainbow in Wind Cave National Park

A RAINBOW

What makes a rainbow?
You need the sun.
You need raindrops.
Sunlight looks white, but
it is not. The raindrops
bend the sunlight. Then
you see all the colors in
sunlight.
You see the colors as a
rainbow.

Rainbow in the Arizona desert after a storm

Now you know about many kinds of storms. Each one is different.

Listen to the weather reports. They will tell you more about storms. They will tell you if a storm is coming.

They usually will not tell you about rainbows. You have to look for a rainbow yourself.

WORDS YOU SHOULD KNOW

blizzard(BLIZ • erd)—a very heavy snowstorm with strong winds

cloud(KLOWD)—a collection of very small drops of water or ice crystals held in the air

crystal(KRISS • til)—a solid thing with sides and angles that form a pattern

drift—to pile up such as snow; a pile of snow blown by the wind

fair weather(FAIR • WEH • thur)—clear and sunny weather

funnel-shaped(FUN • il • SHAIPT)—in the shape of a cone

hail—small pieces of ice that form from rain that falls through very cold air

hurricane(HER • ih • kain)—a storm with very strong winds and heavy rains

lightning(LITE • ning)—a flash of light in the sky caused by a form of electricity

rainbow(RANE • boh)—a half circle of colored light seen in the sky opposite the sun, especially after a rain

rainstorm—a heavy amount of water that falls from clouds to the earth

sleet—frozen or partly frozen rain

storm—a strong wind with rain, sleet, hail, or snow

thunder(THUN • dir)—a noise that is caused by lightning heating the air

thundercloud—a cloud from which rain will fall

tornado(tore • NAY • doh)—a very strong wind that blows in a funnel shape

waterspout—a very strong wind that blows over water and which sucks up the water

wind—moving air

INDEX

About the Author

Ray Broekel is a full-time freelance writer who lives with his wife, Peg, and a dog, Fergus, in Ipswich, Massachusetts. He has had twenty years of experience as a children's book editor and newspaper supervisor, and has taught many subjects in kindergarten through college levels. Dr. Broekel has had over 1,000 stories and articles published, and over 100 books. His first book was published in 1956 by Childrens Press.